# No, *we are not* f♥king there yet...

BONNEY
PRESS

*and other universal truths of parenting*

For all the parents who made so
many sacrifices and wondered if
it was worth it...*

Published by Bonney Press,
an imprint of Hinkler Books Pty Ltd
45–55 Fairchild Street
Heatherton Victoria 3202 Australia
www.hinkler.com.au

BONNEY
PRESS

Author: Andrew Willis
Illustrator: Robin Swift
Art director: Paul Scott
Prepress: Graphic Print Group

ISBN: 978 1 7435 2067 3

Printed and bound in China

*(It was!)

# No, we are not f♥king there yet...

## and other universal truths of parenting

**Andrew Willis • Robin Swift**

# Nursery Rhyme Time

The baby pups turn round three times,
The baby birds don't cheep.
I read the book and I know it said,
Please go the f♥k to sleep.

The baby cats, they softly purr,
The baby mice don't peep.
That book's wrong, maybe nursery rhymes,
Will sing you the f♥k to sleep.

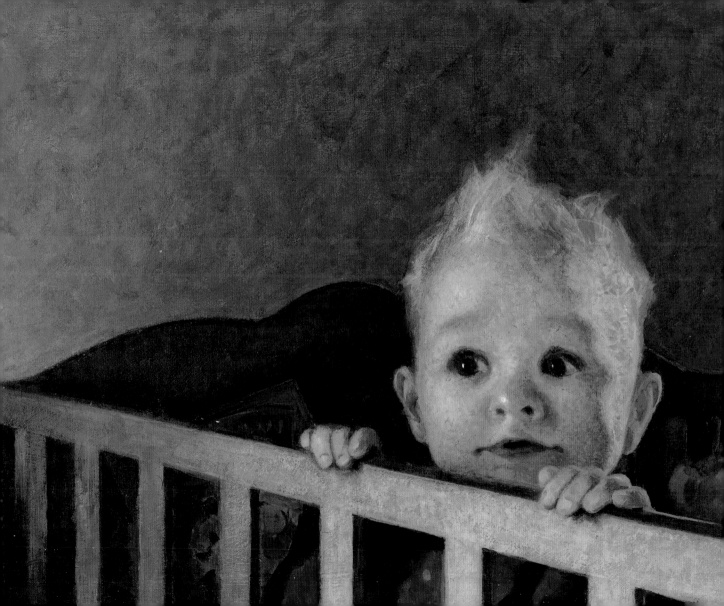

# Power Spew

Bouncing baby on my knee,
Baby smiles and laughs with glee,
Faster bounces, fiddle dee dee,
Now baby spews all over me.

# Playing in the Garden

Playing in the garden, looking at the flowers,
Playing in the garden, staying there for hours.
Playing in the garden, many holes are dug,
Playing in the garden, oh f♥k you ate a slug!

Playing in the garden, that slug has gone right in,
Playing in the garden, with slug guts on your chin.
Playing in the garden, you'd think that I would learn,
Playing in the garden, but no! You ate a worm!

# Push the Shopping Trolley

See Mummy push the shopping trolley,
Gathering food for the pantry,
While you lie on the ground,
Screaming like a banshee.

You won't be quiet, you won't get up,
No matter what I try.
So I make the move to call your bluff,
And leave you there to cry.

Everybody stares at us,
Like they could stop the crying.
I'm begging you, please stop it now,
I feel like f♥king dying.

I pick you up, you scratch my face,
You kick cans to the floor.
We'll starve, who cares, we're going home,
I can't take this anymore.

# Going for a Drive

You're so soft and smooth and cuddly,
I love the way you feel.
Yet when I put you in the car,
You turn to rigid steel.

For me you kick and scream and grab,
You somehow lock your spine.
But oh when darling Grandma's here,
You do it f♥king fine.

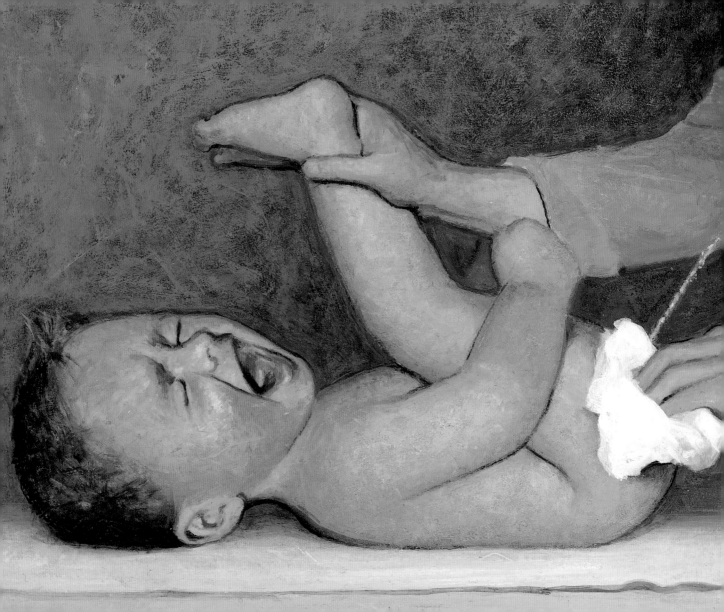

# Changing Baby

Changing baby, one two three,
You have done a lot of wee.
Nappy off,
Wipe you down,
Then you f♥king go to town.

Water flying through the air,
Water flies without a care.
I'm up north,
You're down south,
All your wee goes in my mouth.

Gag and choke, run to the sink,
Without looking grab a drink.
Drink it all,
Gag some more,
Spit the breast milk on the floor!

# This is the Dinner that Mummy Made

This is the dinner that Mummy made.

This is the baby who threw the dinner that Mummy made.

This is the food that dribbled down the wall that was hit by the baby who threw the dinner that Mummy made.

This is the dinner that replaced the food that dribbled down the wall that was hit by the baby who threw the dinner that Mummy made.

This is the baby who threw the dinner that replaced the food that dribbled down the wall that was hit by the baby who threw the dinner that Mummy made.

This is the food that soaked into the brand new f♥king carpet that was hit by the baby who threw the dinner that replaced the food that dribbled down the wall that was hit by the baby who threw the dinner that Mummy made.

This is the Mummy who cried the tears that merged with the food that soaked into the brand new f♥king carpet that was hit by the baby who threw the dinner that replaced the food that dribbled down the wall that was hit by the baby who threw the dinner that Mummy made.

This is the bottle of wine that was drunk by the Mummy who cried the tears that merged with the food that soaked into the brand new f♥king carpet that was hit by the baby who threw the dinner that replaced the food that dribbled down the wall that was hit by the baby who threw the dinner that Mummy made.

# You're My Gorgeous Little Angel

You're my perfect little darling all the time,
You're my perfect little darling all the time.
Two days before a big appointment,
You need antiseptic ointment,
Because you were swinging on the washing line.

You're a treasure chest that's holding untold riches,
You're a treasure chest that's holding untold riches.
We see the nurse tomorrow,
And, much to my great sorrow,
You fall over and need to get some stitches.

You're my gorgeous little angel up on high,
You're my gorgeous little angel up on high.
We're off to see the nurse,
This is like a f♥king curse!
How did you end up getting a black eye?

# The Road Trip

We're going on a road trip, a road trip, a road trip,
We're going on a road trip,
No, we're not there yet.

Because we're in the driveway, the driveway, the driveway,
Because we're in the driveway,
It's pretty f♥king clear.

What's that? Forgot your teddy, your teddy, your teddy?
What's that? Forgot your teddy?
I'm afraid that's just too …

Now you're f♥king screaming, screaming, screaming,
Now you're f♥king screaming,
Dad's gone to get the bear.

No, you can't have lemonade, lemonade, lemonade,
No, you can't have lemonade,
Your water will be fine.

We're in the f♥king house again, house again, house again,
We're in the f♥king house again,
Getting lemonade.

You're feeling like you're carsick, carsick, carsick?
You're feeling like you're carsick?
We're still at the f♥king house!

We'll unpack the car now, the car now, the car now,
We'll unpack the car now,
Let's all go play inside.

# See My Little Darling

See the little elephant holding mummy's tail,
See the little plankton eaten by a whale,
See the little monkey doing a monkey dance,
See my little darling shoving mud pies down his pants.

See the little panda bear high up in the tree,
See the little clownfish swimming in the sea,
See the little kangaroo in its mummy's pouch,
See my little vandal as he paints the f♥king couch.

See the little python slithering on the ground,
See the little chameleon … oops, it can't be found,
See the little baby birds waiting to be fed,
See my little genius with his nappy on his head.

See the little kitten sleeping on its tummy,
See the little lizard sleeping where it's sunny,
See the little lambkin counting all its peeps,
See my little drummer boy who *never* f♥king sleeps.

# No, That Doesn't Go There

Toast in the DVD player, a button up your nose,
Marker on the walls? No, that's not where it goes.

Mud pies on the carpet, a handful of dog poo,
Dirty nappy on the table? Does that seem right to you?

Fingers in the knife drawer, mashed potato in your hair,
Baby in the tool shed? No, you can't go in there.

Mummy knows where these things go, and those are all just wrong,
But all that means to Mummy is they'll be there before long.

# Here Comes the Dinner Plane

Here comes the dinner plane,
Dinner's on its way.
Please, my little angel,
Eat the food I cooked today.

Here comes the dinner plane,
It's got nowhere to land.
You won't eat any food I cook,
But you'll spend hours sucking sand.

Here comes the dinner plane,
Bringing dinner's jewel.
Come on, eat the f♥king food,
This plane is low on fuel.

Here comes the dinner plane,
Bringing food with glee.
Still not eating? F♥k it then,
I'm off to watch TV.

# Learn to Count

One is for this little nose, on your face so tiny,

Two is for your lovely eyes, so big and round and shiny.

Three is for the smiles you give because you love to play,

Four is for how many times you made me cry today.

30 is for the seconds I had to take a shower,

200 is for the decibels of your screaming power.

300 is my heart rate when you ran towards the road,

A thousand is for the times today you dumped a f♥king load.

A million is my blood pressure when you nearly ate the glue,

Infinity, for some crazy reason, is how much I love you.